WHERE'S MY BROTHER?

Henry's daughter

WestBow Press books may be ordered through booksellers or by contacting:

WestBow Press
A Division of Thomas Nelson & Zondervan
1663 Liberty Drive
Bloomington, IN 47403
www.westbowpress.com
844-714-3454

Interior Image Credit: Gail Jacalan

ISBN: 978-1-6642-6209-6 (sc)
ISBN: 978-1-6642-6210-2 (e)

Library of Congress Control Number: 2022905706

Print information available on the last page.

WestBow Press rev. date: 4/6/2022

WESTBOW
PRESS®
A DIVISION OF THOMAS NELSON
& ZONDERVAN

It was a very cold winter..Brrrr! School was finally out for the Christmas holidays. Jake was an 11 year old boy, that lived with his mom and dad, and a younger brother... Micah, that was 4 years old. Micah liked to hang out with big brother Jake, and Jake's friends. Jake really didn't like that, and just put up with little brother Micah and felt he was a "bother..." most the time...but he did what his parents told him to do. One day after a really BIG snow...Jake and his friends were very excited about all the new snow...the snow plows had piled up the snow on the curbside and it was as high as 10 foot tall! Perfect to make a Fort! Jake and his friends got dressed up in their "play Army gear"...and started outside. They took plastic shovels and all else they needed to make a Fort... As he was walking outside, Jake's mom told Jake that his little brother Micah, was going out to play with them and Jake was to watch out for him... augh!

Jake said "ok mom..." but didn't really want to do it. As he started outside he told Micah, "Come on, just stay out of the way...." Jake and his friends began to build their Fort....they shoveled the snow and made tunnels until their hands were frozen.... As they tunneled through the snow it began to look like a Fort inside.... It was the coolest looking Fort EVER!

Just as they were playing in it, Jake heard his mom call out to him to check to where little brother Micah was... Panic struck Jake's heart!

He had not seen Micah for a while...so he started looking for him... he ran through the tunnels and called out for Micah. He could not find him...Jake asked his friends to also look for Micah...

pretty soon all the boys were looking for Micah and calling out his name... running through all the tunnel...no answer! Jake was really scared...he had LOST his little brother! Oh NO!!!! Now he was in big trouble... he yelled out... "Where's my brother?" no answer. Again, "where's my brother? " Please God..."where's my brother"? Jake finally went inside and told his mother that he had "lost his little brother"...

It was the most horrible thing that ever happened...pretty soon the entire neighborhood was looking for Micah....

Jake's mom and dad were going to all the neighbors' homes...asking if they had seen Micah, all said NO, they had not seen him.

Jake and his friends had demolished the Fort...down to a foot high... still looking for Jake's little brother, Micah.

Jake took a break to wipe his eyes...he had been crying and his tears were freezing on his face... his nose was red and frozen...he was so scared and he felt bad, deep down inside...he was really missing his little brother. Jake was in his living room sitting down with his hands on his teary, cold and frozen face....he felt life as he knew it was over! He believed in God and Jesus and got on his knees

and prayed for their help to find his little brother... this was serious! Only they could help... this prayer was important and sincere from his little heart.... he needed God's help to find his little brother...safe... After praying, while Jake was still sitting in the living room...he could hear a faint little noise...like a soft little breathing noise...? What was it? Then he noticed there was a big brown "lump" on the bottom of the coffee table...it was a large, long brown coffee table with a large shelf area underneath ...between the 2 ends...Jake got closer and found that Micah had crawled up in a brown furry and warm throw, underneath the coffee table and had gone to sleep...

Jake was SO HAPPY to see Micah...he yelled for his mom and dad...and showed them Micah's little hide-out...and nap place...and that Micah was safe, thank GOD! Jake was so happy to know where his brother was. He prayed again, thanking God that his little bother was safe. Jake learned a lot that day, to be happy for his little brother.

He also learned to be responsible and do what he is told to do, and MOSTLY...to depend on God and Jesus to answer his sincere prayers...always. Jake now takes more time to play with his little brother and watch out for him...and most of all... he takes time to love his little brother...

About the Author

Author is a Christian Licensed Marriage, Family and Child Therapist for 35+ years, now retired. She is a mother, grandmother and great grandmother. Each story has a moral value and encourages children to be kind and good to others.

Printed in the United States
by Baker & Taylor Publisher Services